Table of Contents

ful woman of God she is today. Taneka hones into aspects of this journey through her own personal experiences, tethered with the Word of God. Each lesson and affirmation in this prolific offering, will assist the reader in the realization of the wealth of happiness and joy that is on the other side of problems, perplexity and pain; to recognize your worth, even if no one else does, and finally, to be assured of the love of the Father for us, to love us into being the very best version of ourselves, not only for ourselves or for our husbands, but for His glory!

Dr. Judith Christie-McAllister

Foreword

Dr. Judith Christie-McAllister

"Wife Lessons" is an honest and transparent gaze into the milestones of the journey towards truly understanding the role of wife, not according to the world's standards, but according to the Word of God. These lessons and affirmations are poignant, thought provoking, mostly convicting, in that they counter the thought of the worlds system, the societal lawlessness, and challenges the wife to move with grace and humility, understanding her primary function as intercessor.

Some portions of this book will serve as a mirror causing the reader to be challenged to tell all the truth about where they are in their walk with the Lord concerning their marriage. Through these affirmations, the reader will come to realize that often, this marriage journey is a death walk; where we must die to ourselves and what we think is best - but in the end, God always resurrects his purpose. For Jesus to be resurrected, he first had to die, and through his resurrection, we now have victory. For us to be the best God has called us to be, we must first die to the image of what we thought marriage should be, so He can resurrect it to be what He desires.

These affirmations will lift you to believe in yourself again, to hope and dream again! Wife - It might be dark in your marriage, but just hold on – weeping may endure for a night, BUT joy cometh in the morning (Psalm 30:5).

For over 30 years, I have watched Taneka grow into the power-

Dedication

I dedicate this book to the woman reading it now. Whether you bought this book, someone bought it for you, or you found it at a garage sale, it is in your hands because it found you.

Holy Spirit

Thank you for curating the pages in this book. Thank you for walking with me and being a guide, counselor, and friend throughout the years. The lessons you've taught me have been invaluable. You have been so patient with me when I chose to do things my way instead of listening to your wise counsel. You corrected me when I was in error and celebrated every small victory. I would not be who I am without you.

I love you.

Requests for information should be emailed to cherubimsong@gmail.com.

Book layout and cover design:
Kimberly Briggs
Kimpbriggs@gmail.com

Wife Lessons

#hiswifehisrib

by Taneka Walston
with thoughts from Tafari Walston

Introduction

Welcome, my sister.

God is intentional with everything He says and does. In the inception of creation, He was intentional. When He created man from the dust of the earth, He was intentional. When he formed woman from the rib of man, He was intentional. God said, "It's not good for man to be alone. Let us make him a helper comparable to him" (Genesis 22:18). He created woman. Eve, the name given to the woman, was intended to be Adam's wife, helper of responsibility, carrier of his seed, and mother of his children. She was to reign with Adam on the earth. She was intended to be a tool in the hand of God to help him build. Instead she unintentionally became a weapon in the hand of Satan to destroy the original plan of God.

When we are first introduced to Satan in the Bible, he is talking to Eve tempting her to eat the fruit of the tree the Lord prohibited them from eating. He caused her to question God's instructions, which

led her to the ultimate deception. She ate the fruit, gave some to her husband and, consequently, forfeited their God-given authority. Now the Good News (the Gospel) is when Jesus died and rose again, He gave us back that authority.

I believe this devotional helps expose the lies and tricks of the enemy as it pertains to your role, responsibility, and authority in your marriage. I pray that something you read heals, corrects, challenges, and causes you to look within. There is no condemnation here, only love. I've been married 20+ years now and I still get challenged in a lot of these areas.

So sister, let's grow together and be who God intended us to be-- #hiswifehisrib.

How to use
Affirmations

When you read the affirmations, insert your name. Declare them over your life daily. The commentary that accompanies each affirmation is there to bring clarity to what's being said.

I suggest you keep a journal nearby to document your journey. Document your mental breakthroughs, your challenges, your grievances, your "ah ha" moments, your "Daddy are you serious?", your good days, and your not-so good days. All of it matters.

Remember, this is a journey. You may have to stay on an affirmation for a week, or even a month. That's perfectly ok, sister. Take your time. Be open and honest with yourself and God. The Holy Spirit is with you every step of the way. You're not alone.

You have sisters that have been praying for you for years.

Extra Notes

His thoughts
Her prayers

I've read many books, sat in plenty of seminars, and listened to a lot of women teach other women how to be better wives. Though I found them to be very informative and enlightening, they all were missing one thing: the husband's perspective. I believe it is important to hear from our husbands and find out what's really important to them. I asked my husband what husbands need from their wives and Tafari's responses can be found on the "His Thoughts" pages.

Now, let me put a disclaimer out there: all men are not the same. So even though you might find some good nuggets, you should ask your husband what *he* needs from *you*. That will keep us from spending years thinking we are getting it right, when we are actually getting it wrong. Take the time to have an ongoing conversation with your husband about his needs, and be prepared because his needs may change over time. If he responds with, "I don't know, babe," and can't ar-

ticulate his needs, ask the Holy Spirit to reveal them to you. If your husband's response is, "Babe you're perfect," then close this book, pass it along to a friend, and start writing your own book (just kidding). Either way check in every now and again to make sure his response is still the same.

Ask your husband what he needs from you and be okay with his answer.

Dear Lord,

Thank you for teaching me and instructing me in the way I should go and guiding me with your eye (Ps 32:8). Thank you for helping me to bridle my tongue (James 1:26). Help me to rightly divide what my husband says to me. Help me not to be easily offended, or so emotional that I misinterpret what he says to me. Help me keep my attitude in check. Teach me how my husband hears. Give me the words that will bring him life. My desire is to be a tool in your hands to build him up; not a weapon in the hand of Satan to destroy him. I trust you with all my heart. I don't lean to my own understanding. I acknowledge you in all my ways, and you direct my path (Prov. 3:5-6).

Holy Spirit, help me to discern what is for me. Help me to take the affirmations in this book and apply them to my life. Help me to identify the areas in my marriage that I need to grow in. Thank you for the grace to change.

Amen

Alright, Sis. You ready?

affirmation

01

When I sow who I am supposed to be in my marriage, I reap who my husband is supposed to be.

The Bible is very clear on the roles and responsibilities of husbands and wives in marriage. For example, Ephesians 5:25 tells husbands to love their wives like Christ loves the church, and wives to submit to their husbands in everything as unto the Lord. Two different roles and two different responsibilities. He loves, and you submit.

Please understand, I'm not saying you will get what you give (apples for apples). Just because you sow submission into your marriage, doesn't mean your husband will submit in return. God does not require your husband to submit to you. Nor does He require you to love your husband like Christ loves the church.

If we settle in our hearts and minds that God's Word is the final say, and that He knows best, it will be easier to do things His way, and in return get His results. In the garden, we see Eve submitting to the enemy, and Adam submitting to Eve, instead of obeying God. I believe this was one reason God had to set order in the relational dynamic of husband and wife.

The order was not set to demean. It was set to protect the entire family structure. Husbands and wives have different graces on their lives. Wives, believe it or not, have a grace to submit and husbands have a grace to love like Christ loves. I know that this may go against everything society says, and may seem foolish and archaic. But didn't God say He would use the foolish things of this world to confound the wise (1 Cor. 1:27)?

When a farmer plants a seed, he doesn't see what is happening underground, but he knows a work is taking place. When that seed is in the ground, it takes on another form and comes up as a tree. When you sow who you are supposed to be in your marriage, the growth in your husband happens "underground" where you can't see it.

You may not see it at first, but be patient, God is working. Even before we see it, change is happening; remember when planting seeds, change happens beneath the surface first.

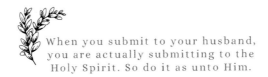

When you submit to your husband, you are actually submitting to the Holy Spirit. So do it as unto Him.

Your Thoughts

_____

_____

_____

_____

_____

_____

_____

_____

_____

_____

_____

_____

_____

_____

affirmation

01

affirmation

02

I exhibit godly character in my marriage.

What is Godly character? Freebiblestudystudyguides.org says Godly character can be defined as "the ability to discern God's right way from the wrong, and to voluntarily surrender one's own will to do what is right in God's sight and, with the promised supernatural help, to resist the wrong even under pressure and temptation."

In Galatians 5:16-26, Paul describes the Works of the Flesh and the Fruit of the Spirit. He advises the believer to "walk in the Spirit, [so] you will not fulfill the lust of the flesh." In this passage he explains that the works of the flesh are evident, and he goes on to list them (see chart). He also lists the Fruit of the Spirit as a template for how to live.

Having Godly character means you resist the temptation to go "tit for tat". You won't say things like, "I'm just giving you the same energy you're giving me" or, "If you can do it, so can I!"

Instead, you show kindness, temperance, and self- control. Don't be sarcastic, condescending, or contentious. Let your words be sprinkled with grace (Col. 4:6).

Having Godly character means being patient with your husband if he's not moving the way you think he should, loving you the way you need, or growing spiritually at the rate you would like.

Having Godly character is controlling your temper in heated discussions and not being attitudinal or sarcastic.

Having Godly character is being who God created you to be in your marriage, even if your hubby is still growing into who God has created him to be.

Having Godly character is apologizing when you're wrong, even if you feel justified.

Having Godly character is responding to situations with faith and not fear.

Everyday we are faced with the opportunity to exhibit Godly character. One way these opportunities show up is in conflict. Depending on your personality type, pride, and ego, exhibiting Godly character in conflict may be challenging–especially if you feel you're always right. I mean who doesn't think they're right the majority of the time? The Bible says,"All a person's ways seem pure to them, but motives are weighed by the LORD." (Proverbs 16:2 NIV).

Culture teaches us that, "a happy wife equals a happy life". I actually hate this phrase because it gives wives permission to have a selfish, manipulative mindset and puts pressure on the husband to do things their wives' way, instead of what they know is right, for the sake of peace in the home. It's reminiscent of Adam heeding the voice of Eve and not God's voice. It tells women that their happiness is the most important thing and that it's the husband's responsibility to fulfill that mandate.

I know it can be difficult at times to be kind if someone (especially your husband) has an attitude. Sometimes you have to be the hero and exhibit Godly character first. Don't wait to do what's right. Just do it! And also don't let the actions of others determine how you move. God rewards openly the things you do in secret.

It's been my experience that however challenging it may be to exhibit Godly character, when I do, my flesh dies, my spirit is strengthened, and God is glorified! So sisters, I encourage you to consult with the Holy Spirit and ask Him to show you areas that you need to grow in. Areas where you think you're right but may be wrong. Ask Him to help you exhibit Godly character. It's challenging, but doable. Trust me, you may not see the effects of your obedience and sacrifice immediately, but change is happening and you will reap your reward!

Your Thoughts

_____

_____

_____

_____

_____

_____

_____

_____

_____

_____

_____

_____

_____

affirmation

02

"...walk in the Spirit, and you shall not fulfill the lust of the flesh." Galatians 5:16

WORKS OF THE FLESH	FRUIT OF THE SPIRIT
Adultery	Love
Fornication	Joy
Uncleanness	Peace
Jealousy	Longsuffering
Outbursts of Wrath	Kindness
Selfish Ambitions	Goodness
Dissensions	Faithfulness
Heresies	Gentleness
Envy	Self-control
Murders	
Drunkenness	

God ensured all the works of the flesh could be overcome by the Fruit of the Spirit.

affirmation

03

"When I submit to my husband, I'm actually submitting to God."

God never looked at women as less than men. He created woman as an answer to a problem that man didn't even know he had. In Genesis 2:18, God says, "It is not good for man to be alone. I will make him a helper comparable to him." The definition of comparable is, equivalent quality; of the same kind. Adam could not reproduce after his own kind without Eve. She was created to help him fulfill his assignment on earth.

After Eve heeded the voice of the serpent in the garden, it revealed her vulnerability to be influenced by the suggestions of Satan, her uncertainty of the word God spoke to Adam, and her ability to influence the man. When they disobeyed God by eating the fruit, a part of them died.

Their spirits were no longer in tandem with God. God then set a new order. For Adam, He implemented the concept of hard work. For Eve, He said, "I will greatly multiply your sorrow and your conception. In pain you shall bring forth children; your desire shall be for your husband and he shall have rule over you." Genesis 3:16 (NKJV). Even though Christ has redeemed us from the curse of the law, God still sets a standard of order in marriages.

In Ephesians 5:22-33 and 1 Peter 3:1-7, Paul and Peter instruct believers on how we are to conduct ourselves in marriage. In both scriptures, they tell women to submit to their husbands as unto the Lord.

For some women, the very notion of submission is inconceivable, to others it's offensive and demeaning. I hear women say things like:

I won't submit to my husband because he's not my daddy.
I'm mad at him.
I'm not letting a man control me.
I'm smarter than he is.
I used to submit in the beginning, but he took me and my obedience to God for granted.
I don't trust his judgment.

Can you relate to any of these responses?

I can understand how wives (including myself) can feel this at times. It seems like we got the short end of this stick:

C'mon, God. Are you seriously expecting me to surrender my will to my husband and give him control over my life? Even if he's not walking upright before you?
God, are you saying that he's always right?
Are you saying I don't have wisdom or discernment to know the right thing to do?

So he can just do whatever he wants and I can only do what he wants?
How is that fair?

Sound familiar? Listen sis, I understand how you feel. But at the end of the day, our opinions and feelings should never override God's word. Even if we don't agree with it.

Satan has used some men (not all) to use scriptures to manipulate and control their wives. To make them feel small and insignificant. But that's not God's intention. God created us equal. He placed His spirit on the inside of us. He equipped us to be the solution, not the problem. We are the gateway from conception to manifestation. For example, we receive our husband's seed, house it, nourish it, and give them a baby.

God sees you and your husband as one. You all are on the same team. Not competitors. God said, "The husband is the head and the wife is the body." (Eph. 5:23). Both are equally significant to the functionality and productivity of the whole. We are to work in tandem like our physical bodies do.

I've also learned that most women only have a problem with submission when it comes to their husbands. We will submit to our bosses, pastors, girlfriends, social media, and latest trends. We will even submit to a stop light or stop sign. It has no power to physically stop our cars. But we respect the authority that has set the laws in place. We understand without the traffic light or stop sign there could be an accident because everyone is headed in their own direction. It brings order, which prevents collisions.

Submitting to your husband is for your protection. God said

when you do it, do it as unto Him. If your husband is a wise man, he will identify your strengths and listen to you in those areas. But you are not the head of your relationship.

If your husband can't make a move without your permission, the relationship is out of order. Yes, there should be discussion before a decision, especially when it involves the family, but he is still the head. If you make more money, he is still the head. If you have more education, he is still the head. If he makes you mad, he is still the head. If he is wrong, he is still the head. If he is an unbeliever, he is still the head. He is the head because of what God said, not because of what he does.

God addresses the issue of an unbelieving husband in 1 Peter 3:1, "Wives, likewise, be submissive to your own husbands, that even if some don't obey the word, they, without a word, can be won by the conduct of their wives." God goes on to explain what submission, chaste conduct, and reverence towards the husband looks like. Although God addresses the husbands in verse 8, I don't want that to distract you. Sometimes we can miss our lesson because we are focused on what others aren't doing.

I want to leave you with this. Submission is not meant to punish you, it's for your protection. Submission is not weakness, it's strength. When you submit to your husband, you submit to God.

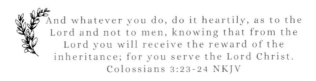
And whatever you do, do it heartily, as to the Lord and not to men, knowing that from the Lord you will receive the reward of the inheritance; for you serve the Lord Christ.
Colossians 3:23-24 NKJV

Your Thoughts

_____

_____

_____

_____

_____

_____

_____

_____

_____

_____

_____

_____

_____

_____

_____

affirmation

03

I trust God with my husband and my marriage.

Do you trust God? I mean, do you really trust God? Do you believe that God loves you? Do you believe that He wants the best for you? Do you believe God brought you and your husband together? Do you believe that what God has brought together, no man can separate? Do you believe in the power of prayer? Do you believe that God hears your prayer? Do you believe that no weapon formed against you, your husband, and your marriage can prosper? If you answered yes to these questions, Amen. But if you couldn't answer yes, my prayer is that you will by the end of this book.

Being a Godly wife takes trust. Sometimes trust is the one thing that has been broken in our lives even before we meet our husbands. We might have been betrayed by loved ones, friends, and even our exes. When that happens it's natural to go into self-preservation mode.

It is quite natural to filter the actions of our husbands through past trauma (heartbreak, betrayal, etc). God wants to heal that place in you. He wants to restore your trust in Him. Now you're probably thinking, "I do trust God. I just don't trust my husband. His actions have shown me that he can't be trusted." I totally understand. But we have to get to the point where we trust God with our husbands.

Not trusting God with your husband looks like this: going through his phone, checking his emails, tracking his every movement, following him around, calling his friends to see if he's with them, requiring him to spend every moment with you because you're afraid that he might be with someone else. Not trusting God with your husband looks like: calling him every five minutes after he leaves the house, being an investigator, waiting to catch him slipping (that's slang for catching him doing something he's not supposed to be doing.)

Trusting God with your husband looks like this: praying for him, asking God to help and heal you in the places where trust has been broken, and walking by faith and not by sight.

Sometimes the things we see don't line up with what God has said. That's when trust kicks in. That's when we war with the word. What we see may be fact, but what God has said or is saying is THE TRUTH!

Satan uses facts to get us to question the truth of God's Word. The only power the enemy has is the power of persuasion. He is a master at using facts to plant ideas in your mind, and your mind can create the perfect scenario for those ideas. God, however, only deals in truth. When truth is revealed about your husband, God calls you to intercede for him.

You have been given authority to transact business in the spirit realm on behalf of your husband. When you intercede you gain insight into the mind and heart of your husband. The information you receive from God about your husband is not to be used against him in an argument. God never reveals information to you about your husband to bring division. He never wants you to be fearful or paranoid for that matter. If God reveals things to you that means He trusts you. Yes sis, God trusts you to pray for your husband. God trusts that you will give Him access to your hurts so He can heal them. He trusts that you will press past your natural inclination to "trust your trauma" over His Word.

The question is...will you trust Him with your husband? Will you trust Him with your marriage?

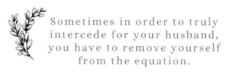

Sometimes in order to truly intercede for your husband, you have to remove yourself from the equation.

affirmation

04

Your Thoughts

_____

_____

_____

_____

_____

_____

_____

_____

_____

_____

_____

_____

_____

_____

_____

_____

affirmation

05

I weaponize the Word of God to fight for my marriage.

I was taught as a child to read my Bible daily. I was taught that the scriptures are holy and that they are the truth. That they are my spiritual food. I was taught the acronym for the Bible is Basic Instruction Before Leaving Earth. What I didn't fully grasp was that it is a weapon, too. Yes, an actual weapon! I read about the full armor of God, but I didn't understand how I could use the Bible as a weapon. It's the sword of the Spirit, but isn't the spirit realm invisible?

Over the years, I learned that the bible was more than a book of stories or sentiments of God's heart. It was more than a decorative piece on the coffee table at Grandmommy's house. It was more than the rule book that we are supposed to govern ourselves by. It is our physical weapon God has given us to fight in the invisible realm.

When you encounter attacks, hardships, seasons of dryness,

distance, etc. in your marriage, don't fight it with emotions. Fight it with the Word of God! Now I'm not going to assume that everyone knows what that means, so here is a working definition. Fighting with the Word is using scripture as your weapon. Finding scriptures in the Bible that pertain to your situation, writing them down (in present tense), and inserting you and/or your husband's name.

For example, Isaiah 54:17 says, "No weapon formed against you shall prosper, and every tongue that rises against you in judgment you shall condemn." Using this scripture as a weapon, for you and your marriage means phrasing it this way: "No weapon formed against my husband, myself, or our marriage prospers. And every tongue that rises against us in judgment is already condemned."

Declaring it in your time of prayer is weaponizing the Word. God's Word is one of our most powerful weapons. The Bible says in Psalm 103:20, that "the angels hearken to the voice of the Word." When you give the Word voice, you give the angels an assignment. Demons are fallen angels that have to obey the Word, as well. When you declare God's Word over your marriage, or any other area of your life for that matter, you activate His will for your life. And His Word is His will.

However, there is one thing that cancels out what you pray, and guess what? It's not the devil. It's what you say. After you're done with your confessions, make sure your daily conversation doesn't contradict what you're believing God to do. For example, if you declare Ephesians 5:25, "My husband loves me like Christ loves the church and gives himself for me," don't contradict that confession by saying to a friend, "Girl, my husband is so selfish. He only cares about himself." You have what you say (Mark 11:23). So even though you spoke (weaponized) the Word of God, your conversation with your friend can cancel it out. Think of it like this, the Word of God is like seeds you plant in the garden of your life. Your negative conversations are like weeds that choke the life of the seed. People are cutting off God's access to their lives by their conversation. If you are praying one thing and saying the opposite, you are deactivating the effect of the Word in your life. God is able, but He works with the power in us (Eph. 3:20)! So let your conversations line up with your confessions.

Complaining about your husband or your marriage is futile. It may be satisfying to your flesh at the moment, but it won't improve your situation at all. It will only upset you more. Complaining puts the nails in the coffin of your current emotional state. Whereas, declaring God's Word frees you and gives you hope. Sisters don't walk away from your marriage in difficult seasons before you've activated your arsenal.

I'm a living witness–this works! Don't relent! Be patient! You may or may not see results overnight. But just like anything we want to grow, it must be watered daily. You water it with your confessions and your conversations. Don't stop! Weaponize the Word...and fight!

Your Thoughts

_____

_____

_____

_____

_____

_____

_____

_____

_____

_____

_____

_____

_____

affirmation

05

I intercede for My Husband.

In the last affirmation we learned how to weaponize the Word and how speaking your confession is important. It's also important that we not only pray for our husbands daily, but truly intercede for them. To intercede is to intervene on behalf of another. When you intercede for someone, you remove yourself from the equation. You move past praying through the filter of your pain or agitation. Your intercessory prayers are not self-serving at all, but sacrificial.

I remember one day my husband asked me if I prayed for him. I was a little offended because most of my prayer time was centered around him. My answer to him was, *"Yes, I pray for you!"* At least I *thought* I was praying for him. The Holy Spirit gently said, "You don't pray *for* him. You pray *about* him. You don't intercede, you tattle."

Don't just pray about things that bother you. Also pray God's will for your husband's life. Ask the Holy Spirit for insight into your husband's heart. The enemy knows if he strikes the shepherd, your husband, he has access to the sheep, your family. (Zechariah 13:7).

Stay in the posture of prayer. Don't allow your emotions to distract you from your assignment. The enemy will do all he can to upset, frustrate, and irritate you. He'll even use your husband sometimes.

When I find myself in my feelings, whether feelings of anger, frustration, disappointment, fear, or even anxiety, worship helps me. I will turn on some worship music and go into thanksgiving. I begin thanking God for my husband. Now I'm not going to lie to you, sometimes I start off with a total attitude. I do, sis. But before I realize it, my heart begins to soften. And what started off as just an act of obedience, transitions into intercession.

Now you may have to find what works for you, but do it. He needs your prayers! He needs your intercession.

affirmation

06

Your Thoughts

_____

_____

_____

_____

_____

_____

_____

_____

_____

_____

_____

_____

_____

_____

affirmation

07

I am my husband's first line of defense in the Earth.

The Bible says God formed Eve from one of Adam's ribs (Genesis 2:22). The function of the ribs is to protect the organs in the thoracic cavity (heart, lungs, and thymus gland), and help push air out of the lungs. They are the first line of defense for our vital organs. In the same way, we have the ability to cover/defend our husband's most vital and vulnerable parts. We cover his heart (what is dear to him), his lungs (his ability to breathe), and his thymus gland (his ability to fight what's toxic to him).

Wow. Even as I was researching the function of these organs, I was so encouraged. I was reminded of how much thought God put into the purpose of a wife. It also encouraged me to know I am multifaceted. But if I don't function as I'm supposed to, praying for my husband, submitting to him, respecting and honoring him, I can be as harmful as a broken rib. Broken ribs can puncture the very organs they are designed to protect.

When I align myself to God's purpose for me as a wife, I am sure to be a tool in His hand to build my husband, instead of a weapon in the hand of the enemy to tear him down.

Be aware: your enemy knows you are the first line of defense, and he will attack you emotionally and mentally. The attack may even come through your husband (unbeknownst to him), by a lack of appreciation, compassion, understanding, and attention. It's difficult to effectively intercede when you are in your feelings. So be mindful not to be too sensitive.

And let me say this, I am in no way justifying toxic behavior or you being emotionally hurt by your husband's actions. What I am saying is don't let your emotions move you off your post. Your emotions have a seat at the table. They just shouldn't be the governing authority at the table. Be led by the Spirit...not your feelings.

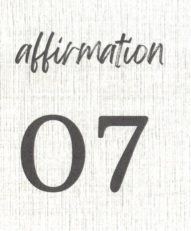

affirmation

07

Your Thoughts

_____

_____

_____

_____

_____

_____

_____

_____

_____

_____

_____

_____

_____

_____

_____

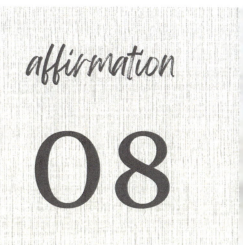

affirmation

08

I see my husband as the finished work God created him to be.

God doesn't start from scratch. He starts from finished. In Jeremiah 1:5, God says he knew Jeremiah and his purpose before he was born. The same goes for you. The same goes for your husband.

If in prayer the Lord reveals somethings about your husband that you didn't know, don't be alarmed. God is giving you insight so you can pray for him. He's not showing you to promote fear or anxiety. It's not to be used as ammunition against your husband, that's what Satan uses it for. Satan is the accuser of the brethren (Rev.12:10). He uses our faults to bring accusations against us. When he does, our advocate, Jesus Christ, reminds the Father of His blood that was shed on the cross.

When God gives you insight into your husband, you are to

respond the same way Christ does and intercede on his behalf. Remind God that the blood eradicated all his sins. Declare what God has said about him. If you don't know, ask God who HE created your husband to be.

Ask Him to open your eyes to see your husband the way HE sees him.

When you do this, He will show you your husband as a "completed man". It may contradict what you see on a daily basis. You actually encounter the work in progress (him still growing and having challenges in areas or not growing at all). Don't respond like Satan would with accusations:

You're not being who God created you to be.
God is not happy with you.
I'm tired of dealing with your foolishness.
Grow up already!

Instead, you should respond by declaring God's word over him and to him:

Honey, you are a mighty man of Valor.
You are more than a conqueror.
Greater is He that is in you, than he that is in the world.
I know God is going to finish the work He started in you.
I believe in you.
I'm rooting for you.

Sis, I want to encourage you. Don't skip over this part. Don't let pride, fear of rejection, hurt, anger, or even complacency stop you from using your words to build your husband up. It may be difficult, and you may say, "I don't want him to think I'm ok

34

with his behavior or decisions. If I don't say anything, how will he know how I feel?"

I want you to implement the tools you gained in Affirmations 4 and 5. This is where you take yourself out of the equation and intercede for him. This is where you allow your words to line up with God's will. Sometimes our feelings will betray us and make us miss opportunities to be used by God in our marriages.

God will never reveal anything to you that you are not graced to handle. You may not think you're graced, but you actually are. You may be challenged, but you are also graced. As a matter of fact, say this out loud:

I am graced for my husband.
I am graced to handle what God reveals.
I am graced to build him up.

And I declare over you my sister, that you will always be a tool in the hand of God that will build your husband up. You will never be a weapon used by Satan to tear him down. If you agree, say, "Amen".

Your Thoughts

_____

_____

_____

_____

_____

_____

_____

_____

_____

_____

_____

_____

_____

_____

affirmation

08

HIS THOUGHTS

Be a Helpmeet

A wife has to be able to help her husband meet the goal at hand: his purpose and his mission. The help she offers needs to be in areas that align with his purpose. She is wired to assist and help him produce the things he is supposed to bring forth in the earth. This means she is there to compliment him, and not compete with him. And she definitely shouldn't be a hinderance to the purpose of God on his life.

Father,

Thank you for my husband. I thank you for working in him Your will and Your purpose in his life. Father, in every season of his life give me insight into him. Help me help him. Help me know who he is to me, and I thank you and appreciate you for the gift that he is.

Thank you for giving me wisdom on how to walk with him. Help me understand his going in and his coming out. Help me understand what You're doing in his life in this season.

Father, I receive the words that are going to encourage him, words of peace and comfort. Holy Spirit, teach me how to sprinkle my words with grace. Help me help him to be who You've called him to be. Help me help him properly steward our family. I bless you in Jesus name, Amen!

I am intentional about showing my husband he is a priority.

Priority: being regarded or treated as important.
-Oxford Dictionary

"If something is a priority, it is the most important thing you have to deal with, or must be done or dealt with before everything else you have to do." Collins Dictionary

Is your husband a priority in your life? In my heart I want to believe mine is based on my intentions. But if I'm honest I can say that my actions may communicate something different at times.

When we first met, I was already active in ministry. My role as a Worship Leader and Director of Worship required me to spend multiple days at church every week. I was also a licensed cosmetologist with a thriving clientele. In the beginning, I would make time to go out on dates with him so

I could get to know him. I would move clients around to free up my time. I would let them know at church that I wouldn't be at every service. He was my priority. Let me be completely honest. My desire to know and be in the company of this tall, chocolate, gorgeous man was my priority.

When we got married, I would do things like, make sure he had something refreshing to drink when he got out of the shower. You see, the shower is his prayer closet, and he spends hours in there. So he would be quite parched when came out.

As our family began to grow, the little bundle of joy whom we both loved deeply, took precedence over everything. Everything revolved around her. When we ate, when we slept, when we went out on dates, etc. My work and ministry schedule revolved around her as well. She became my top priority.

My husband and I still spent time together, and for the most part I made sure he had something to drink when he got out of the shower. You see I said, "for the most part." I will admit there were times that he had to request it because my mind was on the baby or I was just focused on something else at the moment. Sometimes his tone would be attitudinal. I just thought maybe he was warring in prayer.

At the time I didn't even consider that not having what he was accustomed to would cause him to feel disregarded. I also didn't ask the Holy Spirit to give me understanding. Instead, I asked Him to give my husband understanding and patience for what I was dealing with.

The Holy Spirit reminded me that, "Just because I have a baby, doesn't mean my husband doesn't need to be reminded he is a priority." The juice is just one way I chose to show him. With the help of the Holy Spirit, He taught me how I could tend to the baby and still make sure he had his juice. The Holy Spirit showed me that it wasn't about the baby. I was getting so comfortable in the relationship that I stopped being intentional.

If you have children from a former relationship, making your husband a priority can be tricky. Your child or children have been your top priority. By no means am I telling you to neglect your children in any way. Your new family dynamic should be discussed with all parties involved. There should be a clear understanding of everyone's expectations of each other. If that wasn't done before you got married, then asking the Holy Spirit how to proceed is vital.

Ladies, the Holy Spirit is your greatest asset.

Now I can just hear some of you saying:

What about me?
What if he doesn't show me that I'm a priority?
Am I to assume that you want me to bend over backwards to please him?
Why can't he help with the kids?
Am I supposed to prioritize him over my own well-being?

My response is 1 Corinthians 13:4-7. (Also, you can refer to the affirmation on love.)

Prioritizing your husband looks different for every marriage. Prioritizing my husband meant bringing him juice. Yours will be different. I suggest asking your husband what you can do to reassure him he is a priority in your life. When he gives you his answer, hear him out and receive what he has to say. Be okay if his answer is not what you expected. Again, you may need to employ the Holy Spirit to help you balance all of your responsibilities (marriage, motherhood, ministry, business, etc). He will!

I want to leave you with some general examples of how you can prioritize your hubby.

1. Pay attention to him.
2. Create time to bond.
3. Include him in your decisions.
4. Find out his Love Language. (Gary Chapman)
5. Limit your phone time and spend time with him.
6. Take a day off and do his favorite activity.

Sister, the point is, it's going to take intentionality. It's going to take sacrifice. It's going to take help from the Holy Spirit.

affirmation

09

Your Thoughts

_____

_____

_____

_____

_____

_____

_____

_____

_____

_____

_____

_____

_____

_____

_____

affirmation

10

My strong personality is for commerce. It is never to be used against my husband.

Your strong personality and take-charge ways may have attracted your husband, but it will eventually repel him. Use it in business but be gentle with your man. I Peter 3:3-4 says, "Don't let your adornment be merely outward–arranging the hair, wearing gold, or putting on fine apparel–rather let it be the hidden person of the heart, with the incorruptible beauty of a gentle and quiet spirit which is very precious in the sight of God."

At work, when you're in a position of authority, you give commands and expect them to be adhered to. If your employees don't do what you say, they get written up, or their jobs are in danger. When you are in your home, your husband is the head (in authority). If you desire for him to do something, make a request, not a demand. You would never walk in your boss's office and demand anything. You would be mindful of your tone and language. You should show your husband even more respect than you show your boss, and don't speak to him the same way you would your employees.

Let your words always be sprinkled with grace. Don't be combative. If you need help with this, ask the Holy Spirit to show you how you can be more gentle in the way you communicate so you can be effective, understood, and received.

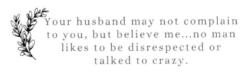

Your husband may not complain to you, but believe me...no man likes to be disrespected or talked to crazy.

affirmation

10

Your Thoughts

_____

_____

_____

_____

_____

_____

_____

_____

_____

_____

_____

_____

_____

_____

_____

affirmation

11

I watch what I say and how I say it.

Have you ever heard the saying, "It's not what you say, but how you say it"? Well, that's only partially true. What you say matters as well.

When I was single, I enjoyed a good debate. I used to pride myself on winning arguments. Since I was talked about in school, I learned how to break people down with my words. I would never back down, even if I knew I was wrong. I wasn't going to let you win. I guess you could say I had a "finisher's anointing". Just kidding. It was all pride and a defense mechanism I was convinced I needed.

When I got married, I had to change that behavior. I needed the Holy Spirit to show me, me. I had to come out of agreement with that carnal mindset. What was once used to protect me, would now have the ability to destroy me and my marriage.

The Bible says, "A soft word turns away wrath" (Prov.15:1). Your communication can be misunderstood just by the tone you use. There is a saying that you catch more flies with honey than vinegar. This doesn't mean to be manipulative or deceptive, just don't be harsh or sarcastic. You don't want your husband to view you as an enemy. If a soft word turns away wrath, a combative, sarcastic word has the ability to incite it.

I understand when emotions are high and you are passionate about what you're saying, speaking calmly, or even graciously may be extremely difficult. Even in the case where you may be hurt by what he did or said, don't hit below the belt by saying things you know will hurt him. In that moment, stop, take a beat, breathe, and ask the Holy Spirit to help you communicate in a way that you will not only be heard, but what you are saying will be received.

Your husband is not your enemy. You both are on the same team. If you enjoy a peaceful home, and want to be your husband's safe place, don't just shoot off at the mouth. Ask the Holy Spirit to be your filter. It may be the difference between being "heard" and being "ignored".

affirmation

11

Your Thoughts

_____

_____

_____

_____

_____

_____

_____

_____

_____

_____

_____

_____

_____

_____

_____

Be Understanding

Wives need the ability to clearly comprehend the heart of the matter. When we study Adam and Eve, we see a clear breakdown in communication. When Eve was tested, she did not communicate what God told Adam. So we can assume that either Adam did not clearly communicate God's instructions to Eve, or Eve didn't see or understand it completely.

This is why understanding is key. The Bible says, in all your getting, get an understanding (Proverbs 4:7). It is vital that every wife understand the nuances of her husband so she can be his proper helpmeet.

Sarah had to understand Abraham's fear of being killed by the Egyptians in order for her to agree to say she was his sister (Genesis 12:13). Most people look at this story as Abraham asking his wife, Sarah, to flat out lie, but she had an understanding that if I don't do this, then my husband will die. Every wife should understand the weight of different situations in order to know how to best respond to get the desired outcome.

52

HER PRAYER

Father,

Father help me to understand my husband. Give me clarity where there is obscurity. Help me to process his words through what he means and not what I would mean if I said it.

Holy Spirit you know my husband and you know me. Help me to hear and understand the call and purpose on his life. If he can't fully articulate or doesn't even know himself, give him clarity and understanding of your call on his life.

Thank you for showing me the role I play in his life and purpose. I thank you that we are one. Spirit ,soul, and body. We move as one. We think as one. You declared that the two shall become one, so I declare, WE ARE ONE!! In Jesus' name, Amen!

There is power in agreement.

Matthew 18:19 says, "Again I say to you, if two of you agree on earth about anything they ask, it will be done for them by my Father in heaven." The word "agree" is *sumphoneo* in Greek. It's where we get the English word symphony. In a symphony you have many different instruments, making different sounds, but coming together for one purpose.

It's the same in marriage. You two have different roles and different responsibilities, but you come together for a common goal. When God sees you coming together, that's when He steps in and blesses you (Psalm 133).

Coming into agreement doesn't mean you start off that way, but that should be the end goal. There may be times where your husband suggests something you know in your spirit you shouldn't be doing. Talk to your husband about it. If he doesn't listen, instead of arguing, go to God in prayer and ask that He explain it to your husband, or that He gives you the right words to explain it yourself. If your husband doesn't listen (to you or the Holy Spirit), release the situation and the outcome into God's hands and trust that He will make sure you're unscathed.

If I were your enemy, it would be in my best interest to keep you and your husband in strife. Your enemy knows that regardless of how great you two are as individuals, if you're in strife, you won't accomplish the purpose God has for your marriage. I admonish you to do your very best not to be contrary to your husband just because you don't understand him/his decisions, or agree for that matter. Again I say to you, pray, pray, pray about it. It may very well be that you need the understanding, not your husband. Either way, when you pray, the Holy Spirit will give you clarity. Reminder: when you and your husband are in agreement, you are an unstoppable force.

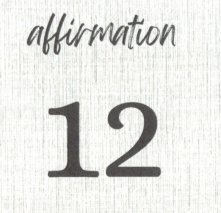

affirmation

12

Your Thoughts

_____

_____

_____

_____

_____

_____

_____

_____

_____

_____

_____

_____

_____

_____

affirmation 13

Even if my husband is not in the place to stand with me, I can agree with God's Word.

I understand that every wife reading this book may not be married to a Christian man. You may not have been a Christian when you got married, so being a believer was never a prerequisite.

Now that you are a believer, you identify that your husband may not possess the tools to cover your family spiritually (yet). The health of your marriage may not be a priority to him. He may be focused on providing for the family. He may be dealing with past trauma, or even current frustrations.

Don't fret. The Bible says in 1 Corinthians 7:14 (NKJV), "For the unbelieving husband is sanctified by the [believing] wife, and the unbelieving wife is sanctified by the [believing] husband. Otherwise your children would be unclean, but now they are holy." Hallelujah! Isn't that encouraging? God knew that you were going to be in this situation. So He made sure he put this promise in His Word for you.

If you feel helpless, you're not! If you feel alone, you're not! God is fighting for you and heaven is fighting with you. When you declare God's Word in faith, you give Him permission to work on your behalf. When you honor your husband, you can win him over.

Also, don't compare your husband or your marriage to anyone else's. Take your eyes off of the seemingly perfect couples on social media. It will only discourage you.

I want to encourage you. If you have been standing on the Word and it seems as if things are not getting better, but worse, Donnie McClurkin pinned a song "Stand". It says, *What do you do when you've done all you can, and it seems like you can't make it through? Well you just stand. When there's nothing left to do, you just stand. Watch the Lord see you through. After you've done all you can. You just stand.*

In Exodus 14, the Children of Israel left Egypt. They came to an impasse. The Red Sea was in front of them and Pharoah and his men were behind them. They had nowhere to go. They were afraid. Moses told them in Exodus 14:13-14 (NKJV), "Do not be afraid. Stand still, and see the salvation of the LORD, which He will accomplish for you today. For the Egyptians whom you see today, you shall see again no more forever. The LORD will fight for you, and you will hold your peace.

For someone, you have been crying out to the Lord for help. You want a sign from Him to know if you should keep fighting or tap out. For someone else, your situation has caused you to approach reading this book with great cynicism. You've been to conferences, prayer meetings, and retreats. You go home fired up, but are met with even more resistance than when you left. They don't tell you it might get worse before it gets better. Well I'll tell you. IT MIGHT GET WORSE BEFORE IT GETS BETTER.

Sometimes you come to an impasse. The enemy and your situation tries to convince you that trusting God by standing on His word won't work. And that you are weak for using your spiritual weapons. So what do you do? I say, stand! Stand on the word. Like Moses told the children of Israel, "The LORD will fight for you, and you will hold your peace." It will take patience, endurance, and faith. But you will see victory!

Oh, by the way, God did perform a miracle on the Israelite's behalf. He parted the Red Sea, they crossed over on dry land, Pharoah and his men went after them, and the LORD closed the sea and Pharaoh and his men drowned.

With God all things are possible. The only thing He can't do is fail.

affirmation

13

Your Thoughts

_____

_____

_____

_____

_____

_____

_____

_____

_____

_____

_____

_____

_____

_____

_____

_____

I don't lean to my own understanding, but in all my ways I acknowledge God and He directs my path.
Prov. 3:6

The mind is a powerful thing. It creates problems and solves them in a moment. It takes us to places without us even leaving the room. It stores our experiences and has endless memories. It's the first place we run to for counsel. It's the one voice we tend to believe is always right. It's always with us. It's the voice we've grown to trust the most. It's always absorbing info, always calculating, always running the infrastructure of our being.

It's important to understand that God wants to be all those things for us. When problems arise, the Holy Spirit wants to be the first we come to. The Holy Spirit wants to be the one we turn to for counsel. He wants us to trust that He's always right.

It's dangerous not to consult Him. The Bible speaks to this in

Proverbs 14:12, "There is a way that seems right to a man, but its end is the way of death."

And Proverbs 16:1-3 says, "The preparations of the heart belong to man, but the answer of the tongue is from the Lord. All the ways of a man are pure in his own eyes, but the Lord weighs the spirits. Commit your works to the Lord and your thoughts will be established." God promises that if we surrender our lives, plans, marriage, careers, children, etc. to Him then our thoughts about those things will be in line with Him.

So how do I apply this to my marriage?

First, you must relinquish control. You must divorce the notion "because I think it's right, it's right." You will need discipline for this, the discipline to reject what experience has taught you, what you may have heard sitting around the kitchen table listening to the matriarchs in your family, or conversations in the salon or even with a close friend. All these things get stored in our minds and subconsciously create a database that the mind uses to explain and resolve issues.

It's okay to listen to friends or women in your family, but their experiences don't always line up with truth. Facts are what your experience teaches you, while truth is what God says about your situation. The only way to know what He says is through His Word and fellowship with the Holy Spirit. Spend time with Him daily and simply ask Him for His input.

Here's a hypothetical situation: My husband came home from work later than normal a few days last week. He was not forthcoming with his whereabouts and seemed a bit agitated, so I did not press the issue. But my mind wouldn't let it go. I thought of my friend whose husband was unfaithful. She said it started with him coming home late from work. Is my husband cheating on me? Stop right there!

I have two options. I can spend the rest of the day or evening creating scenarios (with the help of the enemy) in my mind to support thoughts of infidelity, or I can consult the Holy Spirit on the matter. He will give me wisdom and understanding on how to move forward. As it turns out, there was construction on the freeway that caused traffic to back up.

Think of a situation where you jumped to the wrong conclusion and wished you would have consulted Holy Spirit because it was not what you thought it was. Write down what you would have prayed in that instance. You might need it later.

affirmation

14

Your Thoughts

_____
_____
_____
_____
_____
_____
_____
_____
_____
_____
_____
_____
_____
_____
_____

affirmation

15

GOD FIGHTS FOR ME!!

"...for the LORD your God is He who goes with you, to fight for you against your enemies, to save you." Deuteronomy 20:4

My sisters I want to encourage you today. You are not alone in this. God is with you and He's fighting for you. I'm reminded of the story of the prophet Elisha in 2 Kings 6:8-18. The king of Syria was making war against Israel. He instructed his servants not to disclose the location of their camp. But Elisha, the prophet, sent warning to the king of Israel not to pass that way, helping them avoid the king of Syria's attack. The king of Syria became troubled and thought there was a spy in his camp telling the king of Israel their location. But his servant told him about Elisha, "they have a prophet who tells the king of Israel things you speak in your bedroom." The king of Syria told his servant to find the prophet. They found Elisha and surrounded the city he was in, with horses and chariots while he was asleep. Elisha's servant awoke, saw them surrounded and was very afraid. But Elisha had a different posture. He did not only see with his natural eye, but with his spiritual eye, as well. Elisha told his servant not to fear because "there are more that are for us, than against us!" Then he prayed that the Lord would open the servant's eyes that he may see. The servant's eyes were opened, and he saw that the mountain surrounding Elisha was full of horses and chariots of fire.

Sisters, I know it may look like you're surrounded on every side. Your enemy is closing in on you and you are afraid you will lose your husband, your home, children, job, etc. The enemy has been trying to intimidate you. It feels like you're the only one fighting to save your marriage. But, sister, you are not on the battlefield alone.

Just like Elisha prayed for his servant, I pray God opens your eyes to see that there are more fighting for you than against you. Heaven is backing you up! Keep activating your authority by declaring God's Word over your situation. You activate the Word of God by declaring the scriptures over your life. Find scriptures concerning your situation and insert your name, your husband's name, or even your children's name. The Bible says, "Life and death are in the power of your tongue. (Proverbs 18:21). You have authority!

When you speak the Word, that is prayer. When you pray the Word, you hit your target every time and actually give God permission to work in your situation. Praying your emotions is like shooting a gun with blanks. God draws nigh to a broken spirit (Psalm 34:18), but Satan is not moved by that at all.

James 5:16 says, "The effective fervent prayer of the righteous man avails much." We are supposed to be fervent (having or displaying intensity), but we also must be effective (successful in producing a desired or intended result). So get the Word in your mouth!

affirmation

15

Your Thoughts

_____

_____

_____

_____

_____

_____

_____

_____

_____

_____

_____

_____

_____

_____

_____

Declarations for My Husband

Making declarations over your husband may seem futile, or even a waste of time. I mean, you're going to be declaring things that seem impossible. But faith is believing without seeing. It declares things that aren't as though they are (Romans 4:17).

01 **1 Cor. 7:14**
I declare my husband is sanctified by me, because I am a believing wife.

02 **Matt. 7:7**
My husband seeks the Lord and the Lord is found by him.

03 **Prov. 3:5**
My husband trusts the Lord with all his heart and doesn't lean to his own understanding.

04 **Prov. 3:6**
My husband acknowledges God in all his ways and God directs his path.

05 **John 10:27**
My husband knows Gods voice, hears God's voice, and obeys God's voice.

06 **Romans 8:14**
My husband is led by the Spirit of God and is, therefore, a son of God.

Be Comparable

A husband needs to see himself in his wife. Whether it's in thought, character, habits, or a particular way things are done, it's very important that he sees himself in her.

Let's go back to Creation when God said it was not good for man to be alone. Was Adam alone? Yes, but how? He was surrounded by all God created but he found nothing comparable to himself--nothing that represented himself in the earth. The value of a woman being comparable to a man is the essence of creativity. Unless he sees himself outside of himself, nothing really makes sense. There's a void of self without a comparable partner. Just like God was "alone", though he had heavenly beings all around Him, He didn't see Himself outside of Himself, so He created man–in His image.

In the same way, a wife should be comparable to her husband. She should complement him so they can be the perfect blend of masculinity and femininity; his balance, the other element of himself presented in a different way. Without a comparable wife

most men will fail as a husband. If they focus on how a woman looks and only see her from the outside instead of focusing on whether they see themselves in that woman, they will walk away from their vows. But when a man finds a wife comparable to who he is, he won't just walk away from the marriage. How can a man walk away from himself?

HER PRAYER

Father,

Father thank you for making me comparable to my husband. My prayer is that when he sees me, he sees himself. I lay down who I am to become who we are suppose to be.

Help me Father to hear him when he instructs me. Show me where I've been stubborn, unwilling to bend, and prideful. You have given him the responsibility to wash me with the water of the Word, and to present me to himself a more excellent vessel (Ephesians 5:26-27). Help me not make that hard for him. I thank you, Father, that my husband stands in his authority as the head of this family.

Bless him, bless me, bless our marriage. In Jesus' name, Amen!

Your Thoughts

_____

_____

_____

_____

_____

_____

_____

_____

_____

_____

_____

_____

_____

_____

DAILY
Declarations for You

These declarations are for you and your role as a wife. Take the time to speak these words aloud and over yourself.

01 **I always pray.**
I am not weary in interceding and fighting for my marriage. I reap the fruit of my intercession. I do not lose heart (Gal. 6:9).

02 **I am trustworthy.**
My husband's heart safely trust me. He has no lack of gain (Prov. 31:11).

03 **I am good to my husband.**
I do my husband good and not evil all the days of my life (Prov. 31:12).

04 **I am loved.**
My husband loves me like Christ loves the church and gives himself for me (Eph. 5:25).

05 **I am covered.**
My husband speaks life to me and declares God's Word over me (Eph 5:26).

06 **I am satisfied.**
My husband and I give each other the affection that we need, desire, and want. We don't deprive each other sexually without consent (1 Cor. 7:5).

affirmation

16

Do I want to be right, or righteous?

It's ok to be both at times. But what about those times when you have to choose between one or the other? The word righteous speaks to doing what's right in the eyes of God. You would think that the two words are synonymous since "right" is the root word of "righteous". But they are not.

In marriage, we are faced with choices daily. Are we going to do things our way or God's way? I find God's way is not always the road many choose to travel. You see, God's way tells you to lose your life if you want to save it (Matt 16:25). God's way tells you to bless those that do you harm and pray for those who mean you no good (Luke 6:28). God's way tells you to submit to your husbands in everything as unto the Lord (Ephesians 5:22-23).

Doing things God's way is usually the hardest decision to make, but is actually the most beneficial because it comes with promises. In Proverbs 15:1, the Bible says, "a soft word turns away wrath". But when you're in the heat of an argument, and emotions are turned up, I know you're not thinking about being soft or quiet, but that is actually the best way to be. Because if you would be honest, unless you are just a contentious person, you actually don't even like confrontation, especially with your soulmate/husband.

If you have been sowing seeds of contention, it might take a while for your husband to notice the righteous changes in you, but God notices and rewards it immediately. Remember, our reward comes from God, not our husband's.

affirmation

16

Your Thoughts

_____

_____

_____

_____

_____

_____

_____

_____

_____

_____

_____

_____

_____

_____

_____

Be Submissive

Most people overlook the formation of the word submission. "Sub" means to come under and support. "Mission" refers to an assignment or purpose. The word submission is seen as a curse word in our culture, mostly because it is misunderstood. When wives submit, they are pushing the agenda forward by supporting what the husband is called to do. They do this by interceding and by serving as a compass when their husbands get off track.

Husbands have a mission in life. When we look at Adam's mission in Genesis–to not eat the fruit, to tend and keep the land, and to subdue the earth–Eve was there to come under and support that mission. That's why the enemy came to her, because if he can break the foundation–the support–he can destroy the mission. Adam and Eve's mission was destroyed and death entered them because they obeyed Satan and gave him power.

In Genesis 16, Sarah chose to create her own mission instead of coming under and supporting the mission God assigned to her

and Abraham. As the compass, she changed the direction of their family based on how she thought things should have gone. Her doubt produced a lack of faith and unbelief that led to her creating a plan that attacked the mission God created. Husbands need wives to help keep them aligned with God's plan.

HER PRAYER

Father,

Father, show me where I have adapted the world's ideology concerning submission to my Husband over your Word. I denounce any allegiance to my "own mind and way of thinking" Your Word is the final say.

Help me to understand that you set the order for my protection. Help me to understand that regardless of how smart I am, I am still susceptible to the craftiness of the enemy. I need my husband's covering.

I ask that you would strengthen my husband in the areas where he's susceptible to the enemy because You are his covering. I thank you for the order You set. I know the key is submitting to you first.

Thank you Lord for your truth. Your Word is truth. In Jesus' name, Amen!

affirmation 17

What I bind on Earth is bound in heaven. What I loose on Earth is loosed in heaven. Matt. 16:19

Binding is when an indisputable authority forbids something. Loosing is when an indisputable authority permits something. I'm going to use this as a working definition and insert it in the scripture. Jesus says to us, "I give you the keys to the kingdom of heaven. Whatever you forbid on earth I will forbid in heaven. And whatever you permit on earth I will permit in heaven."

Jesus is the indisputable authority and gives us the authority to transact in the earth. Anything that is contrary to His Word and what He has said to us, we have a right and legal authority to forbid. And anything that we are supposed to see and don't, we have authority to permit.

The enemy wants you to believe that you are powerless. Or that He is more powerful than you. He knows how powerful you really are. You are an unstoppable force and the only one that can stop you, is you! The only power Satan has is the power of persuasion. He works overtime to place images and thoughts in your mind that confirms his strength and your weakness.

Use your authority, sis. Stop complaining about your situation and start declaring what God has said about it. Remember the angels are the reapers and they respond when you give voice to the word of God. When you are binding and loosing, be bold like David when he fought Goliath (1 Samuel 17). Don't let your circumstances or Satan bully you. You have authority and heaven is backing you up.

This is why it is important to read and study the Bible. The scriptures are your bullets and your mouth is your gun. Use your weapons and when you do, don't be timid. Be bold. You're not coming in your own strength. Let's take a page from David's playbook. When he faced Goliath (a giant), Goliath taunted and belittled him. Goliath told David all that he was going to do to him. I love David's response, "You come to me with a spear and a javelin. But I come to you in the name of the LORD of hosts, the God of the armies of Israel, whom you have defied. The LORD will deliver you this day into my hands." (1 Sam 17:45-46, please read the entire chapter.)

When you approach the giants in your life, do it with boldness and confidence. Heaven is backing you up. Stand your ground! Bind and loose! Your victory is inevitable.

Your Thoughts

_____
_____
_____
_____
_____
_____
_____
_____
_____
_____
_____
_____
_____

affirmation

17

Declarations for Your Marriage

These declarations are for your marriage. Take the time to meditate on them and speak them over your marriage.

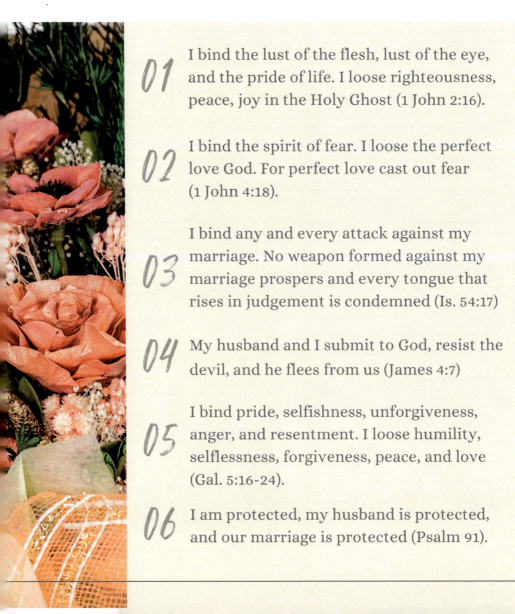

01 I bind the lust of the flesh, lust of the eye, and the pride of life. I loose righteousness, peace, joy in the Holy Ghost (1 John 2:16).

02 I bind the spirit of fear. I loose the perfect love God. For perfect love cast out fear (1 John 4:18).

03 I bind any and every attack against my marriage. No weapon formed against my marriage prospers and every tongue that rises in judgement is condemned (Is. 54:17)

04 My husband and I submit to God, resist the devil, and he flees from us (James 4:7)

05 I bind pride, selfishness, unforgiveness, anger, and resentment. I loose humility, selflessness, forgiveness, peace, and love (Gal. 5:16-24).

06 I am protected, my husband is protected, and our marriage is protected (Psalm 91).

affirmation

18

The flames of intimacy between my husband and I burn brighter than ever before. We love making love to one another.

Sex is not only a physical act, but a spiritual one. It is worship unto God. It's important that you and your husband make love to one another often. I do understand that schedules, children, jobs, hormones, age, health issues, and LIFE, can all play a part in the disruption of the flow of intimacy. The Bible is clear on how important it is to be intimate with your spouse. Intimacy looks different for every couple. I cannot and will not define yours for you. I'm just admonishing you to foster an environment that welcomes sexual intimacy.

If you have been married for quite sometime, if you're not intentional, sex can become mundane. If that is the case for you, ask the Holy Spirit how you can spice things up.

Sidebar: Yes, you can ask Holy Spirit to be your sex coach.

Doesn't the Bible say, acknowledge Him in ALL your ways and He will direct your path? I thought so. Don't be embarrassed to talk to God about your love life. He created it. He knows how beautiful and powerful it is.

God has given us his Word in this area to declare. I want to encourage you my dear sisters. Sex is important! It's not just recreational, or a means to release stress. It's definitely not meant to be used as a weapon, a form of manipulation, or withheld as a form of punishment.

Sex is the natural manifestation of the "two becoming one" (Gen 2:24). It is the one time that you and your husband's bodies are connected. When God made man, He made male and female in one. Then he extracted a bone from Adam and created Eve. They were one and then became two. But when they had sex, they became one again. That's why in biblical days the marriage was not solidified if it was not consummated.

Sis, in a nutshell, if this is an area that one or both of you are dissatisfied in, you have access to scriptures that you can declare to fight in the spirit. Now you're definitely going to have to do something in the natural, too (hint, hint). I can't tell you what that is for your marriage. All I know is that faith without works is dead. Put the work in, sis. At the end of the day it brings glory and honor to God.

If your husband's sex drive is not as strong as yours, or vice versa, you can still pray and declare the Word. Don't be discouraged, sister. God is just as concerned with this area of your marriage, as he is with the other parts.

Your Thoughts

affirmation

18

affirmation

19

I have the strength, patience, and compassion to care for my husband.

This particular affirmation is a last minute entry. This book was in its final stages of editing and formatting. It's September 13, 2022, at 5:49 am (PST).

While I was folding towels and praying, I saw a woman caring for her husband. I couldn't tell if he was terminally ill, or had some form of dementia, but what I do know is she had been caring for him for a while.

Since I've never had to care for my husband this way, I listened attentively as I heard God say, "Tell her I see her and I'm right there with her. Tell her I know she didn't sign up for this (even though the marriage vows state in sickness and in health, we plan for more health than sickness), but I am giving her the patience, strength, love, and compassion to handle this. Let her know I know it gets hard sometimes, and she feels like life handed her a bag of lemons. But sooner than later she will have a tall glass of lemonade."

Hold on, my dear sister. God's got you. He sees you. He sees your tears. He sees your frustrations. All the sacrifices you make daily. The smile you wear when you're really crying inside. You are not alone. I speak peace to you now in Jesus' name. I speak rest to you now. And I say to you on behalf of your husband, "Thank you!"

"So let's not allow ourselves to get fatigued doing good. At the right time we will hatch a good crop if we don't give up, or quit. Right now, therefore, every time we get a chance, let us work for the benefit of all, starting with those closest to us in the community of faith." Galatians 6:9-10 (MSG).

Your Thoughts

_____
_____
_____
_____
_____
_____
_____
_____
_____
_____
_____
_____
_____
_____

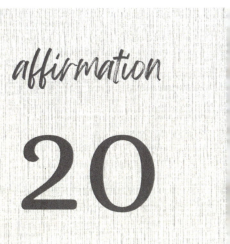

affirmation

20

Even though I may be experiencing hardship in my marriage, I maintain a posture of love according to 1 Corinthians 13:4-8

1 Corinthians 13:4-8 is one of the most recited scriptures at weddings. It's quoted like a beautiful poem that speaks of promised marital bliss. I guess it can make you feel warm and fuzzy inside if you are on the receiving end of that scripture. Have you ever read it from the perspective of the one having to display those attributes? Let's break it down and put it in the context of marriage.

Love suffers long and is kind. Let's just ponder on that for a moment. The very first thing it says love does, is suffer! To suffer is to go through or endure hardship. When you love in your marriage, you may experience hardships, but that doesn't give you the excuse not to be kind. Love is being patient with imperfect people.

Paul, who wrote this passage of scripture under the inspiration of the Holy Spirit, warns that if you love someone, you may experience unpleasant seasons. Marriage is beautiful, and you will experience mountains of bliss, but at the bottom of every mountain is a valley. While you're in the valley, exercise the patience needed to be kind.

Love does not envy. Envy can creep in whenever a wife feels her accomplishments are not being recognized with the same enthusiasm or praise as her husband. Since you are one, there is no need to be envious or in competition. A win for either of you is a win for the team.

Love does not parade itself and is not puffed up. This denotes that love is not prideful, arrogant, or condescending. If your efforts go unnoticed, you might be tempted to sing your own praises, or even diminish your husband's accomplishments to make you feel better about yourself. Don't do that, sis. If your husband is not in a place to see all you contribute to the marriage and household, don't fret, God does. God always rewards openly the things you do behind closed doors (Matt. 6:4).

Love does not behave rudely. Here are a few examples: cutting your husband off while he's talking, rolling your eyes when he says something you don't like, embarrassing him in public or around family, highlighting his flaws in front of friends, belittling him...you get the point.

Love does not seek its own. Love is not selfish, only thinking of your wants, dreams, or desires. It is not thinking of yourself first, and only: where you like to eat, where you want to go on vacation, music you like to listen to, etc. Because you bought into the notion of 'happy wife, happy life', you feel justified in this mindset. Love will consider your husband before yourself. The goal is for you both to compete at putting the other first!

Love is not provoked. (easily angered). Situations may happen in your marriage that bring agitation or even frustration. But I believe this is where we get to exercise the fruit of the Spirit: peace, patience, gentleness, temperance, etc. (Gal. 5:22-23).

Love thinks no evil. No one considers themselves to be evil, but I like the way Rick Renner sums this one up, "Love does not manipulate situations or scheme and devise methods that will twist situations to its own advantage".

Love does not rejoice in iniquity, but rejoices in the truth. Love does not affirm someone in their sin or their false beliefs because love finds no joy in unrighteousness but rejoices in truth. Love never says, "I told you so!"

Love hopes all things, bears all things, believes all things, and endures all things. Love believes the best about your husband and gives him the benefit of the doubt. It does not filter his actions through his past failures. Love is willing to forgive even if he doesn't ask for it. If you notice the word "all" is used in these four areas, so there is no picking and choosing. All is all. Jesus! Let's just take a minute. Take a deep breath, sis. Now exhale. I know, I know...they should ban this from all wedding ceremonies!

Love doesn't quit. It endures through the thick and thin. Culture says that if the relationship doesn't serve me, then I discard it; I'm outta here! I never condone physical, verbal, or mental abuse so I'm not suggesting that if you are in an abusive marriage you should stay in an unsafe environment. But I also never condone giving up on a marriage because you are frustrated, feel there is no hope, or just don't want to do the work.

WHEW! Have you ever just wanted to un-read something in the Bible, and pretend like you never saw it? Now be honest, when you were standing at that altar and hearing this scripture quoted, did you realize what you were agreeing to. Not just receiving it, but giving it as well? I am convinced that the only way this level of love is humanly possible is by the grace of God and help of the HOLY Spirit. I've learned that most of the work that goes into the marriage, is the work on you! It's easy to see the splinter in our husbands eye, but we need to focus on the beam in ours (Matt. 7:3-5). That's why I believe this affirmation is important. It is a reminder that even in the hard times, we can still be loving towards our husbands.

affirmation

20

Your Thoughts

_____

_____

_____

_____

_____

_____

_____

_____

_____

_____

_____

_____

_____

_____

Get ready to put your faith into action! This 5 Day Challenge can be started, restarted, stopped, repeated, supplemented, and more! The goal, though, is for them to be a part of your permanent lifestyle.

Day 01 Write and declare five scriptures you are standing on for your marriage.

Day 02 Post five things you like about your husband on your social media page. If you're not on social media, find a way to insert them into a conversation with a friend or relative.

Day 03 Write five love notes and put them where your husband will find them (sock drawer, medicine cabinet, jacket pocket, etc).

Day 04 Don't fuss, nag, be attitudinal, sarcastic, or negative all day--even if he is. (If you really want to challenge yourself, add this challenge to all the other days.)

Day 05 Post five reasons you married your husband on social media, but make sure you tell him first!

affirmation

21

I walk in forgiveness.

I'm sure you've heard the saying "I can forgive, but I can't forget." I understand the sentiment, but I want to show you why you should, instead of forgetting, choose not to remember. Forgetting happens naturally over time. But choosing not to remember is an intentional act that requires humility, discipline, and love.

When Jesus was asked how many times we should forgive someone, he said, "I tell you, not seven times, but seventy times seven" (Matt 18:21-22).

Then Jesus tells a story about a King who was settling accounts with his servants. One servant owed him 10,000 talents–which equates to about $3.48 billion today. Of course, the servant couldn't pay it. The king was going to sell him, his wife, his children, and all he had to cover his debt. The servant begged for patience and the king was moved with compassion, released him, and forgave his debt. You won't beleive this, but that servant then went and found someone who owed him 100 denarii–around $5,800. He choked the man and demanded he pay what he owed. The man pleaded with him, but instead of releasing him and forgiving his debt like the king did for him, he threw the man in prison until he could pay it.

WAIT! WHAT? Are you serious? Can you believe this guy? How could he not forgive and release such a small debt in comparison to the large debt he was just released from? I know, I know. It doesn't make any sense.

But guess what? We do the same thing. We ask God to forgive our sins and trespasses against Him, but we won't forgive the things people do to us. Even if we are good at forgiving others, we seem to hold a different standard of forgiveness for our husbands. We will forgive our girlfriends, but harbor resentment in our hearts towards our husbands.

When the Bible talks about forgiveness, it's not validating or excusing offenses against you. The fact that Jesus even responds to the question of forgiveness at all, shows his recognition of wrong being done to us.

I remember when something my husband did hurt me to my core. I could feel it in my physical body. I was crying on my bed and the Lord asked me, "Do you not want to hurt anymore?" I responded like anybody would, "Uh yeah, sign me up for relief from this pain!" He responded, "I'm going to teach you how I forgive." Now growing up, I always heard that God throws our sins into the sea of forgetfulness, but that day He told me He casts our sins into the depths of the sea never to remember them. He said, "Baby girl, I keep no record of your wrong." To remember is to relive the memory of that thing. He said to walk in true forgiveness, you will have to stop rehearsing the offense because every time you replay it in your mind, it happens all over again–you feel it all over again. A wound can't heal if you keep picking the scab. God told me, "Release the offense, give it to me. Release your husband from the debt, to make the pain go away."

If we are honest, some offenses can only be healed supernaturally. So even if your husband tried to heal you, all his efforts would not heal the damage done to your heart. You may be saying, "Taneka, that sounds good, but are you saying that my husband shouldn't take accountability for his actions? Does he have full autonomy to move in any way he sees fit with no consequence?" No, I am not saying that!

This is more about the freedom you experience when you are not held captive to offenses. The Bible says if another believer sins against you, go privately to them to point it out. If the other person listens and confesses it, you have won that person back (Matt 18:15-17 NLT). If your husband has offended you and has asked for forgiveness, it is biblical to forgive. In order to walk in forgiveness, you will have to discipline yourself not to rehearse the offense. Whenever the thought comes up, you have to cast down that and any "imagination that exalts itself against the knowledge of God and bring every thought captive to the obedience of Christ" (2 Cor. 10:5). In addition to this, whenever the thought of the offense comes up, you can forgive him again. Verbally say, "I forgive him again."

In the case where there are multiple offenses, like if your husband continues to offend in the same area, you might be asking, "Taneka, am I supposed to forgive him over and over again, or even twice for that matter?" Let me direct you back to the words of Jesus: "I tell you, not seven times, but seventy times seven" (Matt 18:21-22).

My greatest obstacle to truly forgiving is my pride. And every time I choose to forgive the way God prescribes, it kills pride in me.

That being said, please don't take this affirmation and use it as an excuse to stay in a situation where your life is threatened. You can forgive and still leave, in order to stay safe.

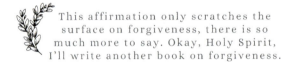 This affirmation only scratches the surface on forgiveness, there is so much more to say. Okay, Holy Spirit, I'll write another book on forgiveness.

affirmation

21

Your Thoughts

_____

_____

_____

_____

_____

_____

_____

_____

_____

_____

_____

_____

_____

_____

Congratulations,

Sisters!

I want to leave you with a few reminders:

- Don't be discouraged because you don't see results immediately. The greatest work has to be done underneath (in the heart) first.
- Don't overlook small victories. I pray the Holy Spirit opens your eyes to see subtle growth in your husband and yourself.
- Give you and your husband grace.
- Identify the enemy in every situation. Hint: it's not your husband!
- Don't filter your "new day" through yesterday's experiences.
- Your memories can be the #1 enemy to moving forward in your relationship in peace and fulfillment.
- Comparison will rob you of contentment.

- Be disciplined in speaking God's word daily (especially on the days you don't feel like it!).
- Don't make any decisions based on your emotions. Emotions have a seat at the table, but they shouldn't be in the governing seat.
- The root of unforgiveness is pride.
- Sometimes the thing that bothers you the most is there to work something in and out of you.
- Watch your mouth! Don't sow weeds in the garden of your marriage.
- Journal your journey. It will be another sister's road map.
- Heaven is fighting for you and with you.
- Sometimes delay is the apparatus God uses to build your trust muscles.
- YOU ARE GRACED FOR THIS!

I love you, my dear sisters!

-Taneka

Testimonials

from wives who have been
shaped by the information
in this book.

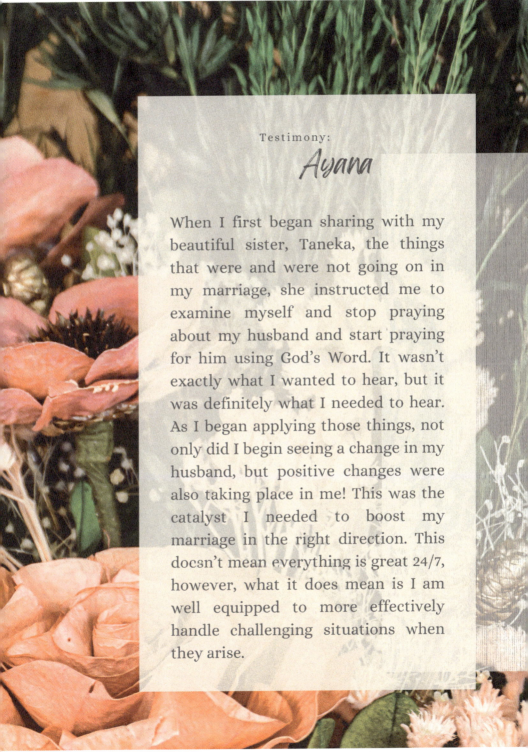

Testimony:

Ayana

When I first began sharing with my beautiful sister, Taneka, the things that were and were not going on in my marriage, she instructed me to examine myself and stop praying about my husband and start praying for him using God's Word. It wasn't exactly what I wanted to hear, but it was definitely what I needed to hear. As I began applying those things, not only did I begin seeing a change in my husband, but positive changes were also taking place in me! This was the catalyst I needed to boost my marriage in the right direction. This doesn't mean everything is great 24/7, however, what it does mean is I am well equipped to more effectively handle challenging situations when they arise.

During the Saturday morning prayer calls she held, I always felt safe sharing extremely personal and sensitive information. Her prayers and genuine camaraderie helped me to not only be the wife my husband needs, but the person God called me to be. I love and treasure these Wife Lessons so much and truly appreciate Taneka for pouring out what has been given to her.

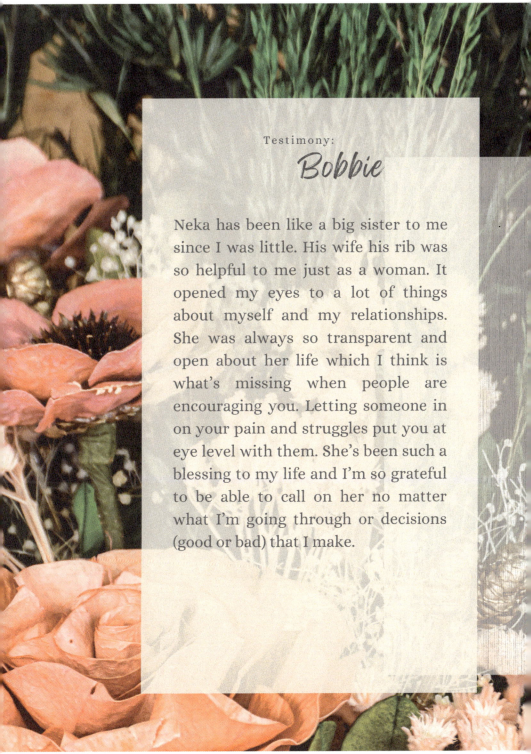

Bobbie

Neka has been like a big sister to me since I was little. His wife his rib was so helpful to me just as a woman. It opened my eyes to a lot of things about myself and my relationships. She was always so transparent and open about her life which I think is what's missing when people are encouraging you. Letting someone in on your pain and struggles put you at eye level with them. She's been such a blessing to my life and I'm so grateful to be able to call on her no matter what I'm going through or decisions (good or bad) that I make.

Testimony:

Brigette

Many times on the [His Wife His Rib] calls God would speak the truth through Taneka. At the time I did not believe my marriage could get any harder but it did. I left the group temporarily but when I came back, the information ministered to me on another level! I stopped doing things in my own strength and I let go of my wrong thinking, my traditions, and superstitions about the love of God. The strong steady support of His Wife His Rib has saved lives because marriage affects the lives of so many people--not just the two that say "I Do".

Testimony:

Dawnesha

In 2020 I was all over the place. I stumbled across Taneka's, Hiswifehisrib prayer group. I was truly ready to walk away from my marriage but I learned that I can work through anything with prayer and supplication. Going to God and asking Him the way to guide me . Taneka and the Hiswifehisrib prayer group helped me and my entire family. I've learned so much about my role and authority as a wife.

Testimony:

Develyn

Taneka is a mastermind in wife lessons. The wisdom she imparts coupled with the experiences she shared ain't for the weak in heart. She is dropping gems that can save marriages and destroy the yokes that keeps satan whispering the wrong messages in women's ears.

Testimony:

F. Ja'Nai

I began seeking Taneka's advice while receiving care for my hair from her blessed hands. Taneka always provided sound nonjudgemental advice from a place of love, experience, and compassion. I'm grateful for the knowledge and wisdom she has shared in preparing me to become a wife and helping to maintain my marriage throughout the challenging times. She has been instrumental in helping me grow as an individual, wife, mother, and friend. I look forward to her perspective on matters!

Katherine

God has not forgotten me. Throughout all the times I have fallen short, Taneka reminded me that God has not forgotten me. I was on the phone with my my mentor and was sharing how hurt, confused, and broken I was from my current situation. She heard me out then asked if she could reach out to a friend of hers who she felt would be able to help me through my situation. That friend was Taneka. Initially, I was skeptical of this woman on the other end of the phone whom I had never seen or spoken to before. After only a few minutes it became abundantly clear that she was anointed for this and God had a divine setup in store for both of us. Taneka spoke into every part of my life in the

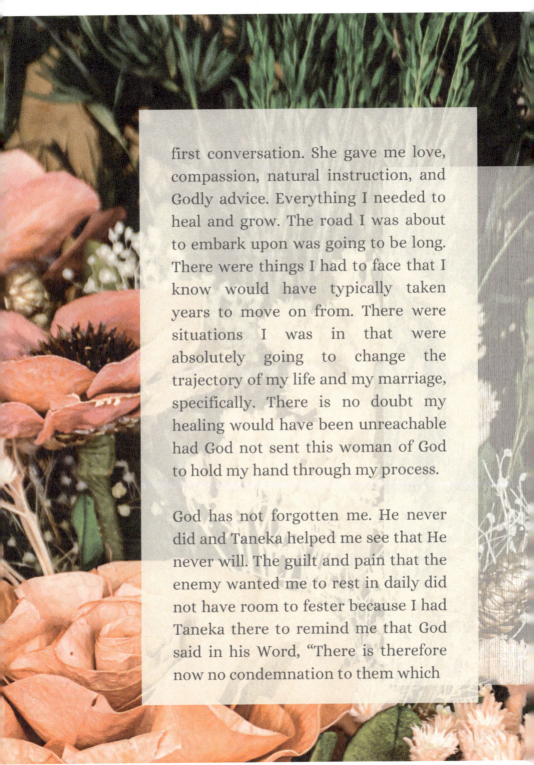

first conversation. She gave me love, compassion, natural instruction, and Godly advice. Everything I needed to heal and grow. The road I was about to embark upon was going to be long. There were things I had to face that I know would have typically taken years to move on from. There were situations I was in that were absolutely going to change the trajectory of my life and my marriage, specifically. There is no doubt my healing would have been unreachable had God not sent this woman of God to hold my hand through my process.

God has not forgotten me. He never did and Taneka helped me see that He never will. The guilt and pain that the enemy wanted me to rest in daily did not have room to fester because I had Taneka there to remind me that God said in his Word, "There is therefore now no condemnation to them which

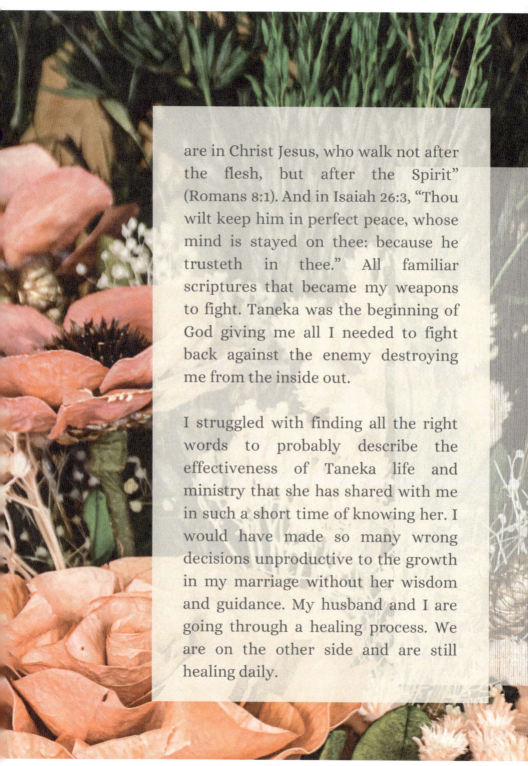

are in Christ Jesus, who walk not after the flesh, but after the Spirit" (Romans 8:1). And in Isaiah 26:3, "Thou wilt keep him in perfect peace, whose mind is stayed on thee: because he trusteth in thee." All familiar scriptures that became my weapons to fight. Taneka was the beginning of God giving me all I needed to fight back against the enemy destroying me from the inside out.

I struggled with finding all the right words to probably describe the effectiveness of Taneka life and ministry that she has shared with me in such a short time of knowing her. I would have made so many wrong decisions unproductive to the growth in my marriage without her wisdom and guidance. My husband and I are going through a healing process. We are on the other side and are still healing daily.

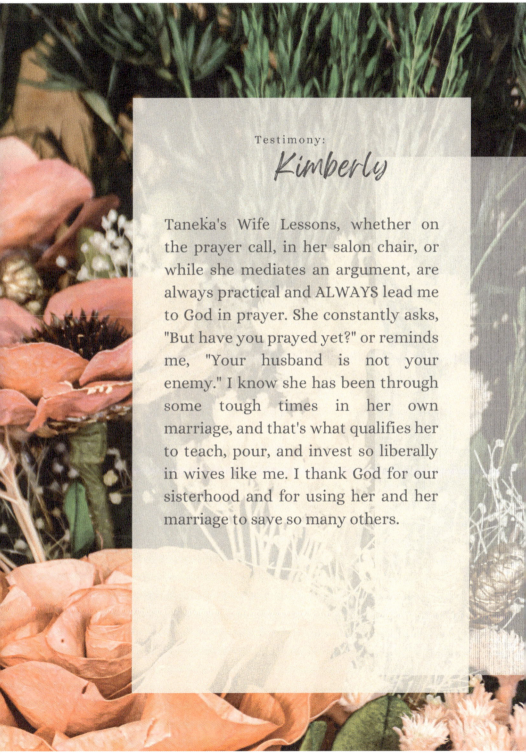

Testimony:

Kimberly

Taneka's Wife Lessons, whether on the prayer call, in her salon chair, or while she mediates an argument, are always practical and ALWAYS lead me to God in prayer. She constantly asks, "But have you prayed yet?" or reminds me, "Your husband is not your enemy." I know she has been through some tough times in her own marriage, and that's what qualifies her to teach, pour, and invest so liberally in wives like me. I thank God for our sisterhood and for using her and her marriage to save so many others.

Testimony:

Latrice

I reached out to Taneka in the middle of a deep depression. My marriage felt like my own personal punishment and hell. I had given everything to my husband and when he depleted me of it all, he sought more elsewhere. Then, he judged me for being hurt and wounded. Taneka has helped me to open my heart and mind to the realities of my marriage. She showed me the mechanisms of the devil, to kill and destroy. She remind me of where my power lies and how to walk in it. My discernment is forever on point.

Somone

The information that I have received from Taneka has been a real blessing. The wisdom & insight she has shared with me has helped me to make needed adjustments to my mindset around dating & marriage. She helps you to hone in on the "areas not often spoken of" in relationships, like what a wife looks like in the spirit versus the natural or what it means when God equates the woman to a rib. This alone has helped me to better understand how to navigate through life's hurdles with my mate. After talking to her I definitely left feeling better equipped for what was to come, good or challenging.

Sonia

When I joined "His Wife His Rib" prayer call over eight years ago, it literally changed my life. No matter what my marriage issue is, Taneka was able to help me tackle it by using the Word of God as a source of reference. Her advice and words of wisdom saved me from walking away from my marriage especially during those pivotal years in marriage when society says marriage is hardest. Not only was she able to assist me in my marriage journey but when my friends and family called me for advice I'd either point them in her direction or give them the same direction Taneka had given to me. Her life and walk with God has been pivotal in helping all the women who's lives she has helped and even changed. I am so grateful to God for her and her obedience to the call on her life.

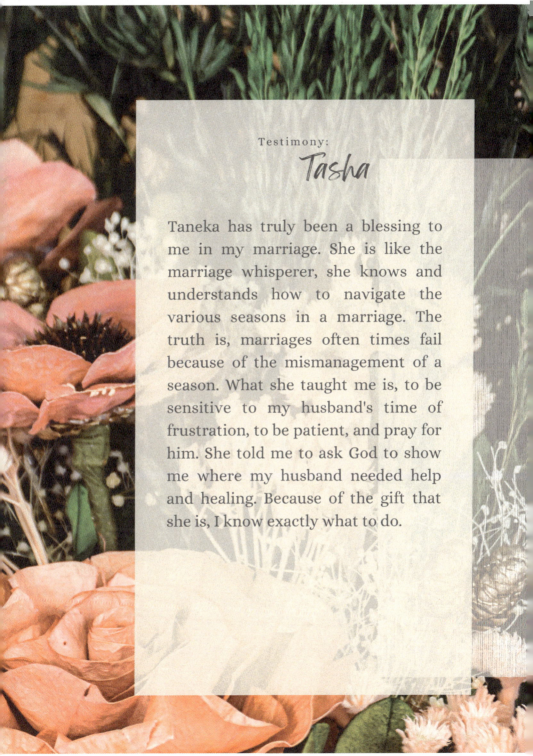

Tasha

Taneka has truly been a blessing to me in my marriage. She is like the marriage whisperer, she knows and understands how to navigate the various seasons in a marriage. The truth is, marriages often times fail because of the mismanagement of a season. What she taught me is, to be sensitive to my husband's time of frustration, to be patient, and pray for him. She told me to ask God to show me where my husband needed help and healing. Because of the gift that she is, I know exactly what to do.

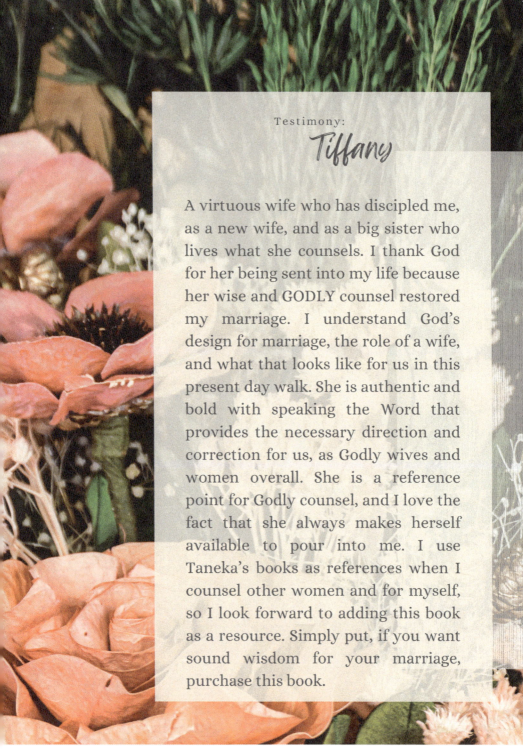

Testimony:

Tiffany

A virtuous wife who has discipled me, as a new wife, and as a big sister who lives what she counsels. I thank God for her being sent into my life because her wise and GODLY counsel restored my marriage. I understand God's design for marriage, the role of a wife, and what that looks like for us in this present day walk. She is authentic and bold with speaking the Word that provides the necessary direction and correction for us, as Godly wives and women overall. She is a reference point for Godly counsel, and I love the fact that she always makes herself available to pour into me. I use Taneka's books as references when I counsel other women and for myself, so I look forward to adding this book as a resource. Simply put, if you want sound wisdom for your marriage, purchase this book.

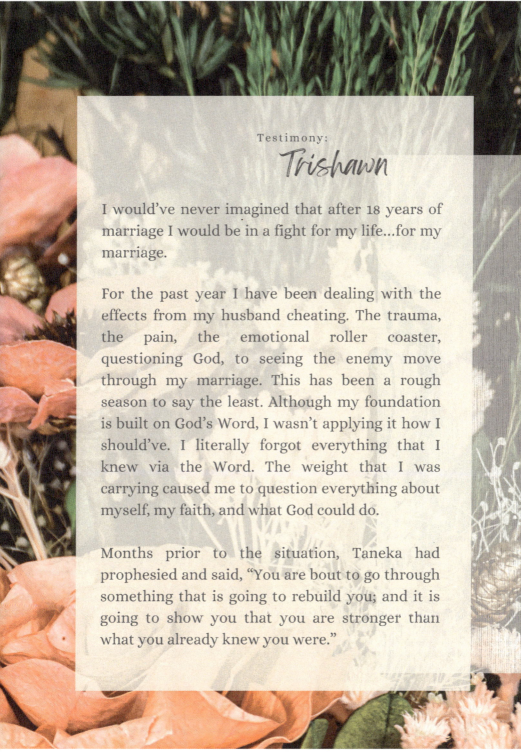

Trishawn

I would've never imagined that after 18 years of marriage I would be in a fight for my life...for my marriage.

For the past year I have been dealing with the effects from my husband cheating. The trauma, the pain, the emotional roller coaster, questioning God, to seeing the enemy move through my marriage. This has been a rough season to say the least. Although my foundation is built on God's Word, I wasn't applying it how I should've. I literally forgot everything that I knew via the Word. The weight that I was carrying caused me to question everything about myself, my faith, and what God could do.

Months prior to the situation, Taneka had prophesied and said, "You are bout to go through something that is going to rebuild you; and it is going to show you that you are stronger than what you already knew you were."

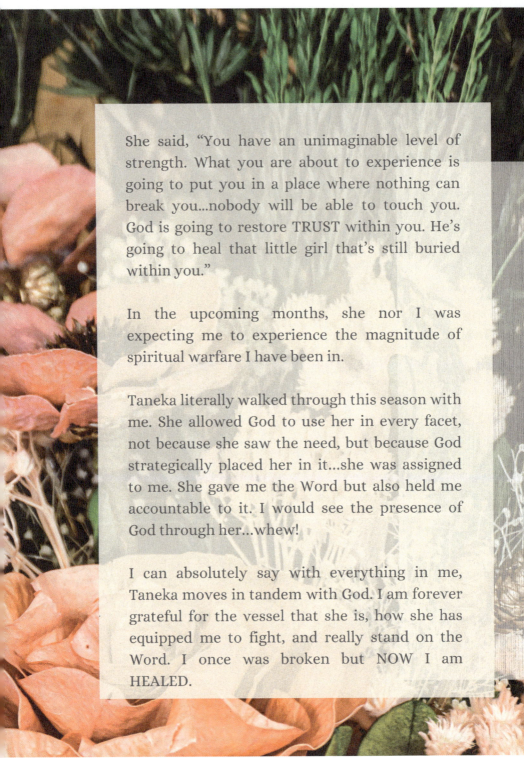

She said, "You have an unimaginable level of strength. What you are about to experience is going to put you in a place where nothing can break you...nobody will be able to touch you. God is going to restore TRUST within you. He's going to heal that little girl that's still buried within you."

In the upcoming months, she nor I was expecting me to experience the magnitude of spiritual warfare I have been in.

Taneka literally walked through this season with me. She allowed God to use her in every facet, not because she saw the need, but because God strategically placed her in it...she was assigned to me. She gave me the Word but also held me accountable to it. I would see the presence of God through her...whew!

I can absolutely say with everything in me, Taneka moves in tandem with God. I am forever grateful for the vessel that she is, how she has equipped me to fight, and really stand on the Word. I once was broken but NOW I am HEALED.

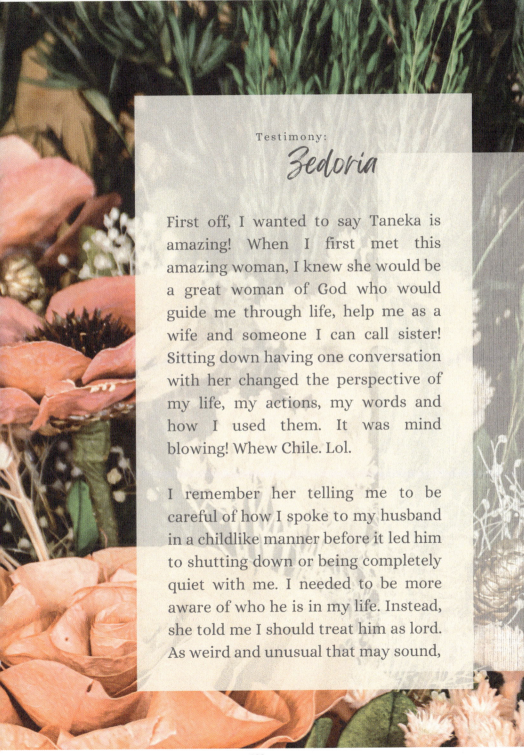

Zedoria

First off, I wanted to say Taneka is amazing! When I first met this amazing woman, I knew she would be a great woman of God who would guide me through life, help me as a wife and someone I can call sister! Sitting down having one conversation with her changed the perspective of my life, my actions, my words and how I used them. It was mind blowing! Whew Chile. Lol.

I remember her telling me to be careful of how I spoke to my husband in a childlike manner before it led him to shutting down or being completely quiet with me. I needed to be more aware of who he is in my life. Instead, she told me I should treat him as lord. As weird and unusual that may sound,

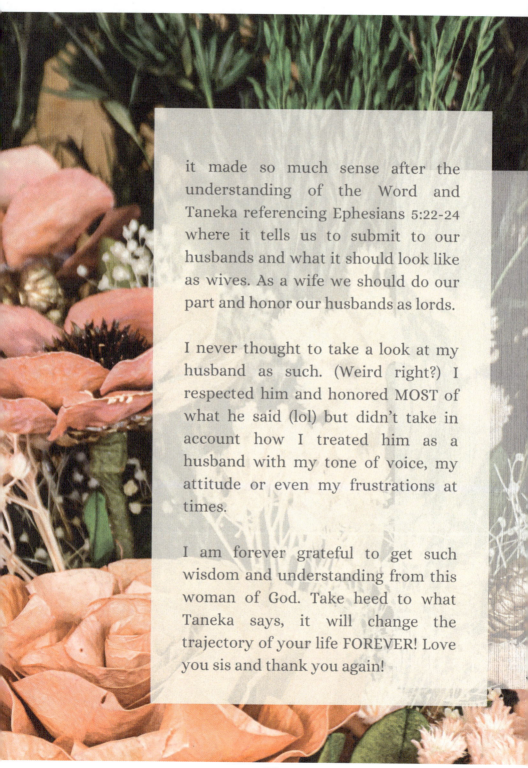

it made so much sense after the understanding of the Word and Taneka referencing Ephesians 5:22-24 where it tells us to submit to our husbands and what it should look like as wives. As a wife we should do our part and honor our husbands as lords.

I never thought to take a look at my husband as such. (Weird right?) I respected him and honored MOST of what he said (lol) but didn't take in account how I treated him as a husband with my tone of voice, my attitude or even my frustrations at times.

I am forever grateful to get such wisdom and understanding from this woman of God. Take heed to what Taneka says, it will change the trajectory of your life FOREVER! Love you sis and thank you again!

about
m e

find
me

for booking
✉ hiswifehisrib@gmail.com

socials
📷 iamcherubimsong

✕ Cherubim Song

f Cherubim Song

websites
- cherubimsong.org
- hydratednhealthy.com

books
- Audience of One: Balancing Devotion & Duty
- Good Morning, Beautiful

WIFE & MOTHER
Proud wife of Tafari for more than 20 years and mother of four beautiful daughters: Sovereign, Virtuous, Shaddai, and Zion. She resides in the Las Vegas area.

SPEAKER & WORSHIP LEADER
A worship leader who has served in ministry for over two decades. Founder of Hiswifehisrib Ministry for wives. Prolific speaker and teacher of all things marriage related and worship ministry.

AUTHOR & RECORDING ARTIST
Author of *Audience of One: Balancing Devotion & Duty* and *Good Morning, Beautiful*. Her debut album and live recording, "It's Time" was received with rave reviews.

STYLIST & ENTREPRENUER
Licensed hairstylist for more than 25 years, she is the founder of Integral Hair Affair. In her pursuit of caring for the health and care of her clients, she created Hydrated & Healthy which promotes the health of the body, inside and out.

Made in the USA
Las Vegas, NV
20 July 2024